FORGOTTEN INDUSTRY AND INSTITUTIONS OF MAINE

TALES OF MILKMEN, AXE MURDERERS, AND GHOST TRAINS

AREND T. THIBODEAU

This book is dedicated to my wife, Christine. Without her unyielding love and support, I would be nothing; without her unrelenting and infallible research assistance, this book would be another two years in the making.

America Through Time is an imprint of Fonthill Media LLC
www.through-time.com
office@through-time.com

Published by Arcadia Publishing by arrangement with Fonthill Media LLC
For all general information, please contact Arcadia Publishing:
Telephone: 843-853-2070
Fax: 843-853-0044
E-mail: sales@arcadiapublishing.com
For customer service and orders:
Toll-Free 1-888-313-2665

www.arcadiapublishing.com

First published 2023

ISBN 978-1-63499-473-6

Typeset in Trade Gothic
Printed and bound in England

CONTENTS

INTROUDCTION: MILKMEN, AXE MURDERS AND GHOST TRAINS

It was early April when I parked my truck to set off on foot and do some exploring. As I headed down the trail, I had not gone too far from where I had parked before stepping in a soft spot on the trail's edge. During springtime in Maine, as the ice melts from the ground everything becomes soft and acts like quicksand, which was exactly what I had thought I'd stepped in when I sunk over my hiking boot in muddy goo. As my right boot filled to overflowing, all I could do was mutter "damn" and press on.

I was determined to walk the couple hundred yards necessary despite my new misery at the end of my leg. I trudged along grumbling to myself, turning left at the trail where I was supposed to and then crossing the stream, surprisingly keeping my other boot dry. A few more steps and I could see the sunlit metal glinting through the trees as I climbed up over the stream bank. I had found them. I forgot all about my wet foot as I pushed through the small patch of trees and they appeared in all their glory, a fleet of milk trucks.

I am an urban explorer. I search for things that have been discarded, abandoned or perhaps (as in the case of the milk trucks) things that have been rendered obsolete. I am drawn to these things by some unexplained reason. Is it curiosity, fascination with the unknown, a penchant for the morbid? I like to think it is all those things, but perhaps also, I like to try and understand loss as it relates to the human condition, find beauty in abandonment, and I enjoy a good mystery.

I document these things with my camera, but not only that, I try to do so in an artistic or emotionally evoking way. That is not to say that each image should speak to you deeply, nor is every image a piece of art, but rather, I think each image should have something to offer to the viewer's interpretation.

As we take the journey together, I will share interesting facts, histories and details about the things encountered in this book. Some items leave behind a plethora of information and some things leave barely a trace. I have tried to include as much information as possible and I have endeavoured to let the images speak for themselves as well.

Although I cover many things in this book, there are a couple of important stories I wish to share and that is why I have used the subtitle *Milkmen, Axe Murders, and Ghost*

Trains. The first and third probably make total sense, more especially when you consider that my first paragraph discusses my soggy sock exploration to the milk trucks, but it is more than just seeing the trucks. It is taking the time to consider what life used to be like when there was no way to get common grocery items into our homes with the ease and convenience that we can today. There is so much more to it than rusty trucks when we consider the evolution of our equipment and examine how we used to conduct ourselves in the industries and institutions of yesterday. It never ceases to amaze me when our modern society is contrasted against the societal conditions at the turn of the century.

I will also talk about Maine's first documented grisly axe murder and visit the jail that housed the killer. The controversial story surrounding the brutal murders may leave you wondering if the killer really did it.

The ghost trains are self-evident. It is difficult to encounter two 90-ton locomotives abandoned in the middle of 3.5 million acres of forest and not call them anything other than ghosts.

It isn't just the trains though; other ghosts will be popping up everywhere, mainly in the form of traces left behind. I do not mean ghosts in the spectral sense, but in the non-literal sense in that these items that have been left behind are ghosts from the past, apparitions of a different time and a different place.

I hope you enjoy my experiences and I appreciate you joining me in my journey. Onward we go!

PART I

THE TRANSPORTATION INDUSTRY

Divco dairy delivery trucks. Divco (Detroit Industrial Vehicles Company) was responsible for most milk trucks on the road at the height of the milk delivery era. The company was started in 1926 and stopped producing trucks in 1986.[1]

1

BY LAND

I grew up with my grandfather being a strong influential role model in my life, and I remember listening with awe as he told me stories of his life experiences and adventures, such as stories of being a ship's gunner during World War II and the less dangerous role of being a commercial driver during the mid-twentieth century. It always enthralled me to hear his tales of the high seas, stories of the open road, and other recollections of his past; delivering milk door-to-door was one of those recollections.

Back before community members could stop into their local convenience store for a quart of milk, the only way they could have the beverage brought fresh into their homes was to rely on the local milkman. It is somewhat difficult to comprehend for those of us who have always been able to pick up a quart of milk anywhere, but there was a time when specialty deliveries were the only way to connect consumers to products such as fresh milk. As my grandfather could relate, this was an era that was reliant on these local drivers. They became part of extended families, receiving gifts or cards for the holidays and becoming part of the daily routine of the families they delivered to. My grandfather would tell me how appreciative his customers would be, especially if he was able to deliver the milk before the coffee was made or the newspaper was delivered.

One day, almost without warning, the pasteurization and homogenization of milk became industry standards. Without going too in-depth about the science involved, it will suffice to say that the process of pasteurization involves heating the milk, and homogenization is a mechanical process that takes place to prevent the cream from separating from the milk. It is a sterilization and bonding process that takes place to stabilize the milk, creating a longer shelf-life and eliminating the need to continuously provide consumers with fresh milk.

Almost overnight the way things were done had permanently changed. A gallon of milk could be transported for many miles and kept for many days in refrigerated trucks. Suddenly my grandfather was looking for work, and fleets of milk trucks were parked, never to be started again.

Aside from being a professional driver and maritime defender, my grandfather also had a life-long passion for automobiles. He would talk about old cars whenever he could, and after his retirement, he ended up working as a caretaker for an antique railroad and auto museum, where he would walk around smiling as he polished fenders on the vehicles. As the steam locomotive could be heard clanking down the track with its whistle blowing in the distance, my grandfather was in his element as he gleefully told all who would listen about the rich histories surrounding each vehicle in his care.

My grandfather was certainly happy when surrounded by old vehicles, and he used to joke to me that he was so knowledgeable about antiques because "it takes one to know one." I always gave him an obligatory chuckle.

Granddad humor aside, each time I encounter an old automobile that has been cast aside and left in a field to disintegrate and rust, I cannot help but think of Granddad, who would be both excited for the encounter and saddened by the state of the vehicle. For those reasons and many others, I want to dedicate part one of this book to my grandfather, the milkman.

This collection of milk trucks represents different milk delivery companies active in Maine during the peak of home milk deliveries.

A fleet of obsolete milk trucks all lined up with no place to go, exposed to the elements and rusting away.

Milk trucks are now sitting in a muddy lot and no longer bringing fresh milk into the homes of Maine residents.

A lone milk truck found in southern Maine. Once a daily sight along its route, now forgotten and used as a storage shed.

Dodge Power Wagon, *c.*1945. The predecessor to the Dodge Ram. The Dodge Power Wagon was manufactured from 1945–1980.

International Harvester KB-6, 1940s. This heavy-duty tow truck was an exemplary working machine in both the pre-war and post-World War II era.

Old Blue. Farm work trucks can be found on many farms in Maine. Some of them still provide farmers with a dependable working vehicle and some now sit quietly in retirement.

Out to pasture. This beautiful farm image would not be possible without this old plow truck and magnificent willow tree.

Snowed in. A retired work truck sits quietly on the edge of a field during a snowstorm in early December.

1939 Chevy Wayne-Body Bus. The Wayne corporation was a leading manufacturer of buses and bus components until it filed for bankruptcy in 1995.[1]

Contemporary mass transit bus. These versatile buses do everything from running inner-city shuttles to transporting passengers coast to coast.

The Buffalo Fire Appliance Company, *c.*1939. The Buffalo Fire Appliance Company began as a maker of fire extinguishers and appliances in 1895. By 1927, the company was building fire trucks from the ground up.[2]

1985 Ford/Farrara 1000/750. Farrara is a contemporary manufacturer of fire trucks which currently employs over 300 workers and has over 150 million in annual sales.[3,4]

2

AUTOMOBILES

In Maine, changes within the auto industry can be evidenced by the vehicles that used to operate on state roads. Auto industry changes are even more astonishing than those of truck and service vehicles. Not only have today's autos become more sleek, less dangerous, and less harmful to the environment, but lost is the pride in craftsmanship and durability.

Chevrolet, *c.*1928–1931. This early model Chevy is very reminiscent of the Ford model T, built during the same period.

Details have been forfeited in today's cars and things are built with replaceability in mind. It begs a person to ponder the notion as to whether we have become a disposable society.

1940 Nash Lafayette. Nash was an independent auto maker from 1916 until 1954 when it merged with American Motors Corporation.

1961 Buick Special station wagon. This family wagon that now sits in retirement was the predecessor to our contemporary minivan.

Packard, early nineteen-fifties. Beginning in 1899, Packard was a luxury car manufacturer in Detroit until it merged with Studebaker in 1958.

1941 Cadillac. The Cadillac has always been the definitive luxury automobile, as this early model demonstrates with its impressive, albeit eighty-one-year-old design.

Buick Super Eight, *c.*1950. The Buick Super series was a full-sized sedan that was made between 1940 and 1958.

1941 Buick Super Eight coupe. The Buick Super series was a full-sized sedan that prioritized consumer comfort and luxury in an automobile.

1949 Buick Super. The Buick Super series was a full-sized sedan that was made between 1940 and 1958.

3

BY SEA

Often people do not realize that all up and down Maine's coast, boatbuilders thrived throughout the nineteenth century and well into the twentieth. Our state nickname, "the Pine Tree State," originated when English colonizers discovered Maine's towering pine trees and declared them perfect for making the center masts of ships for His Majesty's Fleet.

To this day, our most famous shipbuilders can be found at Bath Iron Works. A company established along the Kennebec River in 1884, B.I.W. has been responsible for employing countless shipbuilders in Maine ever since. My grandfather, the milkman, and my father (who once drove an oil truck) both retired from B.I.W.

Roamer, a 57' wooden-hulled fishing vessel, built in 1964. It ran aground over a decade ago after fouling a prop with rope and becoming lodged on the river bottom.[1]

Built at Bath Iron Works during 1937 and Christened the *FV Tide*. The ship was renamed the *FV Squall* and was being used by General Seafoods in 1942 when it was acquired by the U.S. Navy and fitted for naval service. It was commissioned the *USS YP-414* on July 13, 1942.

The vessel was decommissioned on November 13, 1945. Once it was returned to Maritime Commission, it fished out of Rockland Harbor until it was beached along the shores of Penobscot Bay in 1977 to serve as a man-made breaker.[2]

4

BY RAIL

Maine was a tourist destination even before adventurers like my grandfather were gallantly bringing cream into coffee cups across America. Famed for breath-taking scenery and year-round recreational activities, the entire state has always had something to offer.

However, before the family car, everyone had to depend on the railroad to get from point A to point B. If you were a resident of Boston in 1922 and you wanted to go to Moosehead Lake in Maine to do some hunting or fishing, you would have needed to plan the entire trip by rail.

The railroad industry was once so robust that whistle-stops dotted the rail lines as men worked and lived along the rails. These structures were once the pride of the railroads and were elaborately built. Many of them are now demolished and no trace is left behind.

Bodfish Station, *c.*1881. The official residence of the section foreman working for Canadian Pacific Railroad. The building was designed to house the foreman's family upstairs and the downstairs contained an area for those wishing to catch the train, which made its last run in 1960. The building was demolished in 2020.[1]

A substation on an inactive paper company line. Many paper companies had train facilities that resembled large depots with stations, turntables, and their own trackage.

Above left: Maintenance storage building abandoned on an active line. There were once multiple buildings, but most have fallen into an advanced state of disrepair.

Above right: A utility shed among railyard remnants near a non-operational paper mill. Much of the track along with its components have been removed, but some sections like this remain.

Terminal building abandoned on an active line. The now defunct Bangor and Aroostook Railroad administration building can be seen to the right in the background.

Maintenance storage building abandoned on a line that has long since been removed; The building is now privately owned and well maintained.

This passenger station in northern Maine was opened in 1889 by the Canadian Pacific Railway and closed in 1994. This image was taken in 2013.

The station continues to decline in 2022. Windows are now boarded up, signage has been removed, and the roof is beginning to rapidly deteriorate.

5

THE EAGLE LAKE AND WEST BRANCH RAILROAD

I asked my friend Nick if he wanted to go look for the ghost trains of the Allagash with me and he jumped at the chance. Meeting up in Millinocket before the sun was up, we collected our things into Nick's more economic vehicle to head into the woods. From Millinocket we proceeded to the Golden Road, carefully watching for moose as the sun came up.

A person might anticipate a leisurely ride when they imagine what a road with the name of golden might be like to drive on, but that person would be wrong. As the rumor goes, the Golden Road was named sarcastically when it was observed that to build the road from Millinocket to the Canadian border, it would cost so much money that it might as well be paved with gold. The road was completed, and the name stuck, but that was many decades and many logging company transactions ago. Now the Golden Road is an assortment of potholes, varying in depth from an inch to a rim bending, axle-breaking foot deep. If the potholes don't get you down, the several miles of washboard dirt road between stretches of broken paved sections will. Also, if you drive during the week and are attempting to dodge potholes, you will also be dodging logging trucks weighing more than 80,000 pounds and having the absolute, undisputable right of way. The logging trucks are scary and no joke.

If your vehicle's suspension system survives the twenty-mile trip on the Golden Road, the real fun begins when you turn onto the Telos Road. What people do not realize is this part of the state is somewhat lacking in gravel and to maintain the roads in the North Maine Woods, crews use crushed shale to grade and maintain the roads. Crushed shale is like driving on the tips of daggers and if you have thin or otherwise insufficient tread on your tires, you had better bring spares or you'll be stranded in the middle of the woods with a flat and absolutely no cell phone signal.

If you manage to drive the next sixteen miles to the Telos gatehouse without a flat, you stand a chance of making it to the trains. Going an average speed of twenty miles per hour (if you value your vehicle and your life), it will take you well over an hour to go the remaining thirty-six miles to the railroad trailhead. These thirty-six or so miles will be desolate with twisting roads that confuse you with their multiple names and missing signage.

We did finally make it to the trailhead and made the hike into the trains without incident. I want to add that no one should enter the North Maine Woods without back country survival and navigation training. Most importantly, always let someone know where you will be and your expected time of return. The North Maine Woods should never be regarded lightly.

The trains themselves are steam locomotives which were converted from coal to oil burning when they were purchased. This was primarily to avoid forest fires which could be caused by cinders. At the height of their use, these machines moved more than 6,500 cords of wood each week, running day and night.[1]

The railroad was the brainchild of Edouard "King" Lacroix and his Madawaska company. Lacroix was a land baron who specialized in timber operations. He employed over 3,500 workers in the Maine woods working out of more than fifty camps and cutting more than 75,000 cords of wood annually for Great Northern Paper. In addition to being a successful timber contractor, Lacroix also had the skillset of being able to tackle difficult engineering jobs to advance the timber industry.[2]

To be closer to his operations, Lacroix built roads, bridges, and even a dam (Heron Dam which is now known as Churchill Dam) near his headquarters at Churchill Depot. Even though Churchill Depot is now a desolate area of the Maine woods, with only four remote campsites and one ranger station, the area was once a bustling community of travelers, transient workers, and families. To accommodate the volume of people moving through the area, a large boarding house stood on the shore of the Allagash River which could handle many guests at a time. Today, the dilapidated boarding house is all that remains of the once thriving Churchill Depot.[3]

Sometime in the early 1920s, Great Northern Paper Company approached Lacroix with a task to design and build a railroad to carry cut logs from Eagle Lake to Umbazooksus Lake, some thirteen miles through dense forest. Lacroix had a difficult task ahead of him; he needed to get an entire, self-contained railroad to a remote location in the North Maine woods—a feat of engineering in today's modern time, a Herculean task in 1926. Using Lombard Tractors, the workers hauled everything from Churchill Depot, across Churchill Lake, and to the shore of Eagle Lake. Each locomotive weighed nearly 100 tons and workers also hauled the accompanying railroad cars, along with the materials to build a 1,500-foot trestle bridge spanning the north-western arm of Chamberlain Lake, near the Allagash River.

The thirteen-mile Eagle Lake and West Branch Railroad was Lacroix's crowning achievement. He sold the railroad to Great Northern Paper Company just before it began operation in 1927.[4]

Boarding house at Churchill Depot along the Allagash river. If a person were to visit this desolate area of Maine today, it is difficult to conceptualize that it was once a bustling community of foresters and outdoors enthusiasts.

Maine's Ghost Trains of the Allagash. These trains appear ominous when first approached from the trail. It is no wonder how they got their title of ghost trains.

The pictures do no justice to the fact that these trains each weigh more than 90 tons and they had to be hauled through many miles of wilderness before settling here.

Signage along the overgrown track. It is very surreal as you get closer to the trains and the artifacts from the railroad begin to appear.

It is not just the locomotives, but the rail cars and railroad hardware have all been left behind and remnants can be found throughout the area. It's as if train wheel-hubs grow wild in the forest.

At first, only one locomotive and its tender were in operation. It was built in June of 1887 at Schenectady Locomotive Works. In 1928, the second train and tender were purchased.

The two trains were housed in a maintenance shed until it was accidentally burned down in 1969. Shortly after the fire, the trains were painted, and efforts are now being made to preserve them.

The trains seem safe on Maine public lands, but that appearance is deceiving. The trains are still in peril.

The trains are not protected from the ravages of nature, and they also suffer at the hands of vandals and souvenir hunters.

Both trains were discontinued from service in 1933. By the time they reached their end of service, they had become obsolete so the whole line was simply abandoned.

The Eagle Lake Tramway

In 1902, twenty-four years before the Eagle Lake and West Branch Railroad, engineer Fred Dow constructed the Eagle Lake Tramway to reduce the manpower required to move logs across the three-thousand-foot stretch of land between Eagle and Chamberlain Lakes. This was in response to the need to create an efficient way to move logs between the lakes so they could be driven to the Penobscot River via the waterways.[5]

Consisting of 4,800 bolts (which needed to be tightened daily) and 6,000 feet of cable, this was the first of its kind when it was implemented. It was powered by steam and driven by a belt and cable. The rollers in the image begin at the edge of the shoreline and once pulled logs up from Eagle Lake.

The system was driven by a Westinghouse compound engine originally designed for use in electric light plants. The steam-driven system made 255 revolutions per minute with 100 pounds of steam pressure.

The Tramway operated for more than six seasons, effectively moving over one hundred million board feet of lumber before it was discontinued.

6

BELFAST AND MOOSEHEAD LAKE RAILROAD

The Belfast and Moosehead Lake Railroad was a thirty-three-mile track that began in Belfast, passing through stops at Waldo, Brooks, Knox, Thorndike, Unity, and Winnecook, before going on to Burnham Junction in Waldo County. At Burnham Junction, passengers would connect with the nationwide rail network by way of Maine Central Railroad. Ironically, the railroad bearing the moose insignia never came within 100 miles of the Moosehead Lake region where the lake's namesake mammals are more plentiful.

Despite its deceiving name, the railroad thrived not only carrying passengers but transporting goods as well. The trains carried sardines, timber, and even the daily mail. In the days before the milk trucks, the trains also carried fresh milk.

The railroad was commissioned in 1867 and built at a cost of $25,900 per mile. Its first scheduled run was conducted on December 23, 1870. The railroad was the result of thirty-five years of determination, perseverance, planning, and construction. The railroad became a success, but there were controversies and political strife. The railroad did not see its own independence until 1925 when it was released from a lease it had been bound to by Maine Central Railroad. During its first year as an independent line, it carried nearly 112,000 tons of freight and 43,000 passengers.

During the Great Depression, the railroad struggled as annual passenger traffic dropped to under 5,000 with commercial goods dropping to less than 50,000 tons. The railroad continued to struggle until a 1946 decision to replace steam engines with diesel locomotives. The new, more efficient engines brought the company a great deal of success until regular passenger service ended in 1960. Still, the railroad continued to deliver freight until the late 1980s, and it saw some passenger resurgence in the nineteen-seventies. However, that was not enough, and since 1989, trains now only run for excursions.

In 2005, the main rail yard in Belfast had its last train leave the station, the tracks were removed in 2014, and now no trace of the main yard remains.

Today, a non-profit preservation society in the town of Brooks works to preserve the remaining line.[1]

The only remaining section of track between Belfast Station and City Point Station. City Point Station is now a museum.

A General Electric diesel 70-ton switcher, #51. It was purchased in 1946 when the railroad switched from steam locomotives to diesel-powered engines.

A structural remnant on approach to City Point coming from the Belfast terminal in the town of Belfast; no trace of the Belfast terminal remains.

A B.M.L. freight car sits on an unused stretch of track. City Point Station and museum can be seen in the background.

A passenger car sits outside an abandoned rail yard. The black B.M.L. moose head insignia can be seen on the side of the car.

An abandoned freight car on an unused stretch of track near the Brooks Station. The railcar has not moved for some time. Neither the car nor the track seems serviceable any longer.

7

THE BANGOR AND AROOSTOOK RAILROAD

The Bangor and Aroostook Railroad was chartered in 1891 with operations from 1894 until 2003. The railroad monopolized northern Maine with over 800 miles of track covering a distance from Bangor to Van Buren. Even though the railroad served only rural Maine, traveling sparsely populated areas with its biggest city stop being Bangor, the railroad still thrived with the help of Maine's timber and potato industries.

In 1963, its inventory of rolling stock included two passenger cars and 4,646 freight cars—evidence of how heavily the railroad relied on freight for revenue.

The railroad has seen many different owners and many different attempts to survive. It struggled when it stopped transporting potatoes in the 1970s. A decline in the timber industry further exacerbated the problem and the railroad was declared bankrupt in 2003.[1]

The Bangor and Aroostook Railroad headquarters building was once a magnificent office building at the company's main terminal. The heart of its operations now sits abandoned with the windows boarded up.

A Bangor and Aroostook freight car sits alongside Belfast and Moosehead Lake passenger cars in a storage yard in central Maine.

Bangor and Aroostook freight cars which appear to have been sitting idle for decades blend in well with the autumn colors in Maine.

This Bangor and Aroostook freight car sits abandoned by itself, with no other rail artifacts nearby, miles from any existing tracks.

The track has been removed on both sides of these B.A.R. freight cars as they stand a quiet vigil in the woods. Only the section of track that the cars sit upon remains.

8

MAINE CENTRAL RAILROAD (1862–1981)

After chartering in 1845, operations began on the Maine Central line in 1862, and it quickly became the longest line in New England.

In 1917, it had 1,358 miles of track when the United States Railroad Administration temporarily nationalized the line, taking control of it during World War I.[1]

The Maine Central Railroad controlled the trackage of The Belfast & Moosehead Lake Railroad from 1871 until December 31, 1925, due to a fifty-five-year lease. The years of control by Maine Central was rich with political controversy and Belfast eagerly gained control of its line on January 1, 1926.

By the end of 1970, the railroad had 1,183 miles of track and reported over 900 million ton-miles of revenue freight. The Maine Central Railroad remained an independent line until it was bought and dissolved in 1981.[2]

Abandoned trestle bridge of the Somerset Railroad. In 1872, the Somerset railroad operated in the western Maine region of the state. It was absorbed by Central Maine Railroad in 1911 and continued to operate until 1929.[3]

A Maine Central freight car sits abandoned in a defunct terminal area now used for storage and salvage.

This water tower was erected by Maine Central Railroad sometime in the early 1900s. Water towers to supply locomotives with water could once be found in numerous areas, each placed ideally along the tracks in locations such as stations or junctions.

A Maine Central Railroad freight car sits in the back of a line of rail cars which are all being overtaken by nature.

9

GHOSTS ALONG THE TRACK (REMNANTS)

All down the line, businesses like the Black and Gay Cannery used to stand along the tracks to gain easy access to shipping lines. The plant canned many things during its heyday including clams, succotash, brown bread, and blueberries. Canning at the plant ceased in the early 1970s, and the property was sold. Today, most of the building has collapsed.

The remains of Black & Gay Cannery looms in the quiet stillness of the woods near a Belfast and Moosehead Lake Railroad line.

The Republican Journal of Belfast wrote this about the cannery in an article on October 27, 1921: "It is safe to say that there is not a better canning factory building in the state of Maine as nothing was left undone which would in any way weaken its structure."[1]

The J. H. Weymouth wool company began in 1902 along the Maine Central line. The location along the railroad line was perfect for the carloads of western sheep pelts that would arrive annually for processing.

After a year of operations, Weymouth sold his company to the Swift Company of Boston and the factory came to be known as a branch of Consolidated Rendering of Boston. The company continued to be a success employing many workers in the area.[2]

Telegraph Poles

Telegraph technology was developed around the same time as railroads; utility poles were also often referred to as telegraph poles.

Used until the late 1960s or early 1970s, telegraph poles held a multitude of lines, each representing a circuit; each station or terminal would have a telegraph operator that would relay the messages to the crews.

Railroads would also sell wire service to the public during this era, and the news of the day would be sent via wire. Still today, when we hear of breaking news, it is often presented to us as just "coming over the wire"—a phrase held over from the days of telegraph communication.

Roberts and Schaefer Coal Tower

Built by Roberts and Schaefer in Chicago, this coal tower is a monument to a century of fossil fuel burning as it stands a quiet vigil on the edge of a central Maine railyard.

This single coal tower which stands on the west side of the terminal was once used to supply coal to the engines that hauled freight around the state. On the east side of the terminal, a twin tower once stood, and that tower was used to supply coal to passenger service trains. During the years of usage, the two towers were linked together by a conveyor belt that rose above the trains.

The remaining portion of the east coal tower stands to the left in this image beside the abandoned Bangor and Aroostook Railroad administration building.

Above left: The west tower looms in the foreground, seemingly skeletal amongst the barren trees. The Bangor and Aroostook railroad administration building can be seen in the background.

Above right: The west tower and its adjoining utility shed stand a silent vigil on an abandoned track as it waits for a phantom train.

More Ghosts Along the Tracks

An unidentifiable passenger car sits on an unused stretch of track in central Maine. Much of the train car had been vandalized and stripped of parts.

A lone freight car on an unused stretch of track in central Maine. The car is advertising train rides on the Maine Coast Railroad, which was owned by the Maine State Department of Transportation. It closed its operations in December of 2000.[3]

An inactive turntable once used to rotate locomotives. The location was once an extremely active paper mill near the mouth of the Penobscot river. This table has not turned for many years.

PART II

THE MANUFACTURING INDUSTRY

Like the Black and Gay Cannery and Weymouth Wool, many manufacturing plants and factories constructed facilities with easy access to railway shipping lanes. It stands to reason that when the railroads began to fail, the companies that relied on them to ship goods and receive freight also began to struggle. The manufacturing industry, like the railroads, has seen significant changes in the state of Maine over the last two centuries.

Deserted mill, *c.* 1880. This mill produced woolen textile products throughout most of the nineteenth century. In 1973, it began to be utilized as a yarn production facility which continued for more than two decades until the mill was simply abandoned. The town foreclosed on the property in 2009.

10

HYDROELECTRIC POWER

In Maine, one of the easiest solutions to rural electricity supply was hydroelectric power. In the early days of Maine industry, before corporate power companies began to monopolize on large power grids, mills and factories would generate their own power. Before automation and centralized facilities like we see in our contemporary world, each power station had to have its own ability to maintain the system and keep the lights on.[1]

In the early days much more maintenance had to regularly be performed, requiring maintenance facilities where workers could be based to maintain the system. Now automated, localized technology has removed the necessity for workers to constantly be present, and many such facilities have closed.

The exterior of a turn-of-the-century hydroelectric maintenance facility, located near a dam that used to be controlled and operated by a paper company. Even now, this building is striking inside and out.

The interior of a turn-of-the-century hydroelectric maintenance facility. The interior is strikingly done in its woodwork and craftsmanship, quite unlike utilitarian buildings in our contemporary world.

11

MILLS AND FACTORIES

Erected at the turn of the twentieth century by Diamond International Match Company and built alongside the Maine Central line, this mill produced more than just match splints during its nearly 100 years of operations. Toothpicks, clothespins, croquet balls, and more were hewn from raw wood in this mill. The proximity to the rail lines ensured timely deliveries and access to resources.[1]

Erected by the Diamond International Match Company, this sprawling wood-working facility made many wood products and was located along the rail lines in the heart of Maine's timberland.

A panorama of the saw sharpening room inside the plant. Tools and saw blades have been left in place since its closure.

Raw materials left at the plant were wide ranging from small blocks of wood to larger cuts. Each was staged in different areas in accordance with what was being made.

Above: Some materials were round, others square, and different types of woods were present as well. There were a significant number of materials left behind.

Right: Wooden clothespins were scattered about in one area of the plant, presumably the station where they were made. I found it curious that there was a demand for this type of clothespin as recently as 1993.

Left: The plant was unable to adapt to industry changes and it was closed in 1993. Workers left the plant as though they would be returning to work the next day.

Below: The entire facility was demolished in 2022 and all that remains today is an empty clearing along the rail line.

These boilers used to be part of a wood products mill built in 1912 along the shores of the Kennebec River. Producing small wood products at first, it changed ownership around the time World War II was coming to an end; it then built Bristol boats until the mid-1970s.[2]

Inside a woolen mill erected in 1880. Like many mills during this era, it was erected on the water to utilize the hydraulic power provided by nature.

In the early days of manufacturing, mills and factories would be built along rivers and streams to capitalize on the power of water and aid in the manufacturing process. Unfortunately, early practices led to contamination and pollution of Maine's waterways and now waterways are given substantial zoning restrictions.

Stacked lumber can still be found on shelves, as well as tools and equipment needed to operate this lumber yard which was in operation from 1978 to 2010.

Above left: Industrial fans used for ventilation and sawdust extraction now sit idle. The entire mill and its acreage sit quietly surreal, like a ghost town.

Above right: Only a gentle breeze turns these industrial fans now, and the saws no longer cut wood.

A lone wheelbarrow with a flat tire stands guard over the empty lumber yard. The entire facility encompassing several acres and half-a-dozen buildings has been dormant for more than a decade.

Above left: Stairway in a hydroelectric maintenance facility. Turn-of-the-century craftsmanship is evident even in utilitarian buildings such as this.

Above right: A door left open decades ago allows snow to drift into this wood processing mill in central Maine. Built in 1912, the mill made small wood products at first and it then built Bristol boats until the mid-1970s.[3]

Above left: American Woolen Mill electrical supply station. The woolen mill where this electrical panel is located was built in 1850 and won awards for the cashmere it produced.[4]

Above right: Downeast Maine sardine factory, various owners, 1881–1973. Sardines were an important staple in the diet of many New Englanders for generations. These tasty little fish were canned in a variety of ways along the Maine coast from the turn of the century until the 1970s when Maine's sardine industry collapsed.

12

STONEHENGE OF MAINE?

As I was driving along a desolate dirt road in rural Maine, I caught glimpses of a large granite structure, so I stopped to investigate. After a short walk through the woods, I discovered several granite structures tucked in the forest.

My curiosity was piqued. I needed to know the history of this location, but I could find very little information. Even after extensive research, I kept coming up empty handed. The local historical society marvelled at what I had discovered, but they were just as dumbfounded as I was. I continually found myself back to square one each time I thought I was closer to unraveling the mystery. How did these structures end up in a desolate and secluded area of Maine?

If it were not for a town elder, I may never have been able to unravel the mystery. The eighty-three-year-old historian told me it used to be the location of the Black Sawmill which supplied wood for shipbuilding in the nearby coastal community. It was further revealed that a ship built in the area was christened *Bark Black* after Herbert Black, who was the proprietor of the mill. The mill was active in the late 1800s and quickly fell into ruin when operations ceased.[1]

These structures are not visible from any paved roads and strikingly appear as you are strolling through the forest.

Looking downstream. The pillars resemble some sort of monuments at first glance. They presumably supported the mill's structure when it was in operation.

Looking upstream, it begs one to ponder the notion if this stream was much more of a robust waterway at one time.

PART III

INSTITUTIONS

Over time, many industrial practices have grown and flourished in the state of Maine. Others, like the milkman or the whistle stop, have vanished entirely. Likewise, state institutions have seen vast changes in their structures and methods of operation.

The county jail has sat virtually undisturbed since it was forcefully closed in 1975. Considering the walls were painted prior to the jail's closure in 1975, it stands to reason that the peeling paint may contain hazardous lead.

13

JAILHOUSE BLUES

In 1832, Alfred was on the move; the small Maine village had just become a full-fledged shire town, and despite taxpayers complaining of its nearly $8,000 price tag, a stone jail was designated and built in the place of the town's existing "log jail." According to an 1833 legislative report, the wooden jail had become "grossly insufficient and unsuitable for the purpose for which it was built."[1]

Despite the town having their stone jail, it was quickly outgrown as the community continued to grow and prosper. It was decided that the jail was still inadequate for the needs of the quickly growing community and out of necessity, the 1872 legislature approved the necessary funds to build a new jail using the existing location and structure.

It all sounds like standard local politics, but during March of 1873, as the jail was nearing completion, something significant occurred. On March 6, 1873, as most of the world slept, a man entered a home on Smuttynose Island and attacked three women, killing two of them. The third woman managed to escape and was responsible for bringing the killer to justice.

After being woken in their home by an intruder, Karen Christensen and her sister-in-law, Anethe, were slaughtered on their property while the men of the household were out on an overnight fishing trip. Both women were brutally murdered by an axe-wielding man who entered the home sometime after midnight. A broken clock at the murder scene revealed that the murders took place sometime around 1:00 am that morning.

The crime may have gone unsolved if it were not for Karen's sister, Maren, who was also present on that fateful night. Maren was able to elude the attacker after surviving an attack herself and escaping into the night. She hid barefoot in the jagged rocks of the shoreline wearing only her nightgown. She survived the night enduring dangerously cold temperatures with only the family dog for warmth until she was discovered around 8:00 am the next morning by neighborhood schoolchildren. Once Maren was saved, she began to share the grisly details of how family friend Louis Wagner attacked them, cleaving Anethe's head open with an axe and bludgeoning poor Karen. It was the most heinous of crimes, a suspected robbery gone wrong.

The trial of Wagner lasted nine days and it took jurors fifty-five minutes to return the guilty verdict for which he was hanged on June 25, 1875. Many doubts were left as to Wagner's guilt, even after the trial and execution. Even though Wagner had a weak alibi, he would have had to row twelve miles across open sea from the mainland in New Hampshire out to the island. Then, he had to make the return trip, again rowing twelve miles back to shore. A stolen dory in the area was evidence enough to convince the authorities when they discovered its newly installed oar pins showed signs of significant wear in one night. This was coupled with the fact that Wagner was a fit man capable of making the round trip by rowboat. Wagner had opportunity, knowledge, and ability. Was that motive enough to row out to sea in the middle of the night to attempt to rob this house? The jury thought so, and the eyewitness testimony of Maren sealed the deal.

As if that were not enough of this story, there is more. When Louis Wagner was captured for the crime in Boston just days after the murder, he was taken to Portsmouth, New Hampshire, where community members (made up of primarily fishermen) created turmoil as they threatened to take justice into their own hands and lynch Wagner. Reportedly, armed Marines had to be summoned from the nearby Naval yard to quell the hundreds of angry protestors intent on lynching Wagner.[2]

There was also a jurisdictional contention; the offshore Isle of Shoals where Smuttynose is located boarders both Maine and New Hampshire waters. It was ultimately decided that Wagner was to stand trial in Maine, and he was sent to the new secure facility in Alfred on April 29, 1873.

In addition to being its first tenant, Wagner was also one of the jail's first escapees when he absconded with two other inmates on a Wednesday evening in June. It would be three days later before Wagner was recaptured in New Hampshire.

It was not the slyness of Wagner alone that enabled him to escape. In the years following Wagner's escape, more escapes were common. Despite the jail being new and despite all the money that had been spent on its construction, the locks were easily manipulated by the prisoners. Even after the locks were sent away to Boston to be repaired, escapes continued to occur. The last escape from the jail took place in September of 1974 when four inmates climbed through the ceiling and out onto the roof, lowering themselves three stories to the ground with rope fashioned from blankets.

The jail's inadequate security was perhaps a contributing factor for its demise when a riot broke out in the facility in September of 1975. Sparked by the death of a fellow inmate, rioters tore out sinks, bunks, and fixtures. Heavy damage was caused to the jail's infrastructure before rioters were brought under control by more than forty law enforcement officers and others, including firemen with high velocity hoses.

After the riot and the destruction of the facilities, the jail was ordered closed by the courts and the prisoners were sent to be housed in a neighboring facility.[3]

Third-floor west wing. It is uncertain if the color schemes in the jail played a significant role in its design, but the walls in the jail were striking with the differing colors on each floor. When the jail was newly done, it must have been very impressive.

Third-floor east wing. After rioting prisoners destroyed much of the jail's infrastructure, it was closed, never to be opened again. In this image, the tin ceiling is beginning to deteriorate, and the jail is showing advanced signs of decay.

Above left: Fixtures, toilets, and bunks were torn from the walls during the riot. The amount of damage done to the jail was enough to condemn it.

Above right: Sink fixtures, a bunk and a toilet seat are all missing, and something has been torn from the wall—evidence of the riot that has been left since 1975.

Right: Ground floor, west wing. Even now, forty-seven years after the jail's closure, it still feels desolate; a person can easily gain a sense of what it must have been like to be incarcerated in this facility.

Left: Second floor, west wing. The blue color on this floor coupled with the peeling paint and rusty cell doors all work together to create a beautifully surreal scene.

Below: During his escape, Wagner had placed a decoy of himself in his cot and fooled the guards who took hours to discover he was missing.

Above left: Despite the expense of the jail and numerous attempts to fix them, the locks were easily manipulated by prisoners which resulted in multiple escapes.

Above right: The ravages of time and moisture have brought bricks down from the ceiling. Fortunately, this occurred when no one was in this holding cell.

Escapes were much more common before closed circuit television and electronic locks became industry standards. For the guards or warden to keep track of the prisoners, they had to watch them physically. The warden's quarters (which adjoins the jail) was designed with peepholes so that the apartment's occupants might look out anytime and observe the activity in the cellblock.

The facility housed both male and female inmates, and although they were all housed in the same building, the women's detention area was segregated from the rest of the facility. This image is a portion of the women's detention cell where the bunks were located.

View from top floor (attic). Perhaps it is my fear of heights, but I had a difficult time imagining what it would be like to rappel down three stories using only bed sheets.

Women's detention cell. This, and the previous image, make up the entirety of the women's detention area which was separate from the main prisoner population.

Above left: Remains of warden's quarters. Only brickwork and wallpaper remnants remain of what used to be adjoining living spaces for the warden and his family.

Above right: The color schemes in the adjoining living spaces were warm and inviting as opposed to the authoritative, institutional colors inside the jail.

Left: Wallpaper remaining in the adjacent quarters. It is easy to differentiate the administrative areas of the adjoining quarters with the living spaces. It is as though more feminine and decorative choices were made with wallpaper selections in the living spaces.

Below: Wallpaper remnant. In contrast to the previous image, this is a wallpaper remnant from the administrative area of the building. The wallpaper is much more symbolic of authoritative and official décor.

14

HOUSES OF THE HOLY, SCHOOLS & MEETINGHOUSES

The penal institutions in Maine are not the only institutions that have seen tremendous changes over the years. Our social institutions have gone through significant changes as well.

Since the days when we were hunter-gatherers, we have always been social animals. We have a strong sense of communal self that is as old as our anthropological history. When colonial settlers established colonies in New England, it is no surprise that the first structures to be raised were churches, meeting halls, and community gathering places such as taverns.

Churches were so much more than places to gather and worship during scheduled worship times. These were also places used for education, town meetings, and even festivals and celebratory events. The town would use the central gathering areas as places to come together to address the economic, political, or other social interests of the community at large.

Many churches closed during the late nineteenth and early twentieth centuries. The ability for people to travel greater distances to attend larger churches, the internet, and the large townhall have all contributed to the demise of the small-town church.

The churches, schools, and other facades I have selected in this section no longer function as originally intended. Many of them have now fallen into private ownership, some have become dilapidated, and others have been destroyed. Where applicable, I will provide what information I have been able to collect.

Left: I was not able to uncover any data on this church. It was in an advanced state of decay when I discovered it in 2020, and it was demolished in 2022. An interior photo appears later in this chapter.

Below: This church is in an extremely rural part of Maine and records are unavailable. This church has been almost totally grown over with vegetation.

Right: The same church as in the previous image viewed from the back. Despite the church being in an advanced state of neglect, the bell was still located in the belfry.

Below left: Roman Catholic Church, *c.*1919. This modest church is a far cry from the elaborate detail of other structures held by the papacy.

Below right: Community church built 1910. Town records are unrevealing as to any detail in the history of this church located near a small fishing village in Maine.

Left: Memorial Chapel, *c.*1912. All we were able to discern was this church's build date; no other record seems to exist.

Below left: An excerpt from the town's history where this church is located states: "The Baptist people used to hold meetings in the schoolhouse years ago, but in the year 1896, they built a fine church in the village."[1]

Below right: First Baptist Church, built 1832 and remodelled in 1879. This church was originally built in Gothic Revival architecture; the 1879 remodel transformed the tower and its flanking entrances to more closely resemble the Italianate style buildings built in the mid to late 1800s.[2]

Above left: Built in 1870 as School district 8, Bush Schoolhouse. Used as a school, church, and meeting house, it is now privately owned with an uncertain future.

Above right: This church that sits quietly amongst the wildflowers was once the district Sunday school, Ford Chapel Full Gospel Church, *c.* 1931.

Right: Methodist church, 1865. This historic church fell into private ownership in 2020. The town condemned the building in January of 2022, citing the dilapidated and hazardous condition the structure was in. After the owner failed to meet the demands of the town to secure the building, the church was razed on July 13, 2022.[3]

Above left: First Baptist, *c.* 1900. During an interview with the town clerk, it was stated that tax bills sent to church headquarters long after the church had gone dark went unacknowledged. As a result, the town was able to gain ownership of the church. Not much else known as there are no records.

Above right: Methodist Episcopal Church 1892. Again, the history and records of this church are very unclear. It has been in private ownership for quite some time and data is unavailable.

Interior of the church from chapter introduction, structure now demolished. Note the tin ceiling, stained glass, and hardwood flooring. The church was well-built in its day.

Built by the Calvin Baptist Church and Society 1873–1875. Town records are unrevealing as to any detail in the history of this church located in western Maine.

Glad Tidings Church from 1950–2008. Town records are unrevealing as to any further detail in the history of this church.

Built 1902 by the American Baptist Association. Town records are unrevealing as to any detail in the history of this church located in Downeast, Maine.

Built 1840–1870 (record is unclear) as a union meetinghouse for three denominations that shared it. Inactivity and lack of attendance forced it to close in the 1940s.

In an ironic twist of fate, parishioners who once sought solace in being buried next to this church are now presiding over its decay.

In The Dark. The town has grown and developed around this church since the late nineteenth century. The community that the church once helped to strengthen and unify now ignores the building as it stands alone in the hustle and bustle of town. Organized in 1866 by the Church of the Messiah, this church was erected in 1869 and the first service was held on March 6, 1872.[4]

Above left: Sold to the school district in 1960 by the "inhabitants of the town." Records prior to 1960 are unavailable.

Above right: Union Meetinghouse, 1841. It is not difficult to see why the large meetinghouse went away in Maine. According to the United States census statistics, in 1840, when this church was being built, its town had a population of 1,427. The population peaked in 1870 with 1,540 residents. Contrast that to the 2020 census which listed the town's population at 952.

Schoolhouse built in late 1800s. Town elders shared with me a story of a ten-year-old boy, who had the chore of lighting the woodstove every morning to adequately heat the schoolroom by the time classes began.[5]

The Freewill Baptist Religious Society sold this church on June 3, 1899; the record of deeds is lost prior to 1899.

Community Grange #551 chartered November 19, 1925. No longer active. Grange membership and Grange halls have declined in Maine in the last century. Going from 55,212 members and 419 halls in 1907, to 126 halls with just over 4,000 members in 2015.[6]

This Congregational Chapel was deeded June 3, 1884. Town records are unrevealing as to any further detail in the history of this church.

The Solon Meetinghouse built in 1842, Gothic Revival style architecture. The interior is decorated with sixty-six-year-old wall and ceiling frescos.

15

THE SOLON MEETINGHOUSE

If you travel along the Meetinghouse Road outside the small village of Solon, this gothic revival meeting house stands at a crossroads. It is well off the beaten path and this structure has stood in this spot for 180 years. Built on a budget and within modest puritan standards, its builders stipulated that it remain open for public, albeit benevolent and moral use, during the week as well as on Sundays. Since 1842, it has remained open.

For nearly 100 years it served as a church and town hall, but then it began to deteriorate. It was partially restored in 1939, but due to lack of interest in the project, it was never completed and continued to fall into disrepair.

In 1951, the building was given a reprieve from deterioration when students from a local art school created frescoes, floor-to-ceiling, in the building's interior. These works were inspired by the chapel frescoes of Italy and were done in the ancient style using pigment and water, then applying it to plaster before the plaster dries. This essentially allows the artwork to become part of the wall rather than images painted over the surface of it.

Maintaining the religious fundamentals of the building, the students created the frescoes between 1951–1956.

The building and the artwork within are now preserved by the local historical society which was incorporated in 1956.[1]

View from lefthand street entrance. The frescos are simply breathtaking when entering for the first time. The meetinghouse still contains the original 1842 pews.

View from righthand street entrance. The frescos are simply breathtaking when entering for the first time. The meetinghouse still contains the original 1842 pews.

There are two organs inside the meeting house. One is located on each floor. The second floor is only a partial floor with bench seating and the second-floor organ.

The view on the first floor from the organ looking toward the pulpit. This perspective allows unobstructive viewing for most of the frescos.

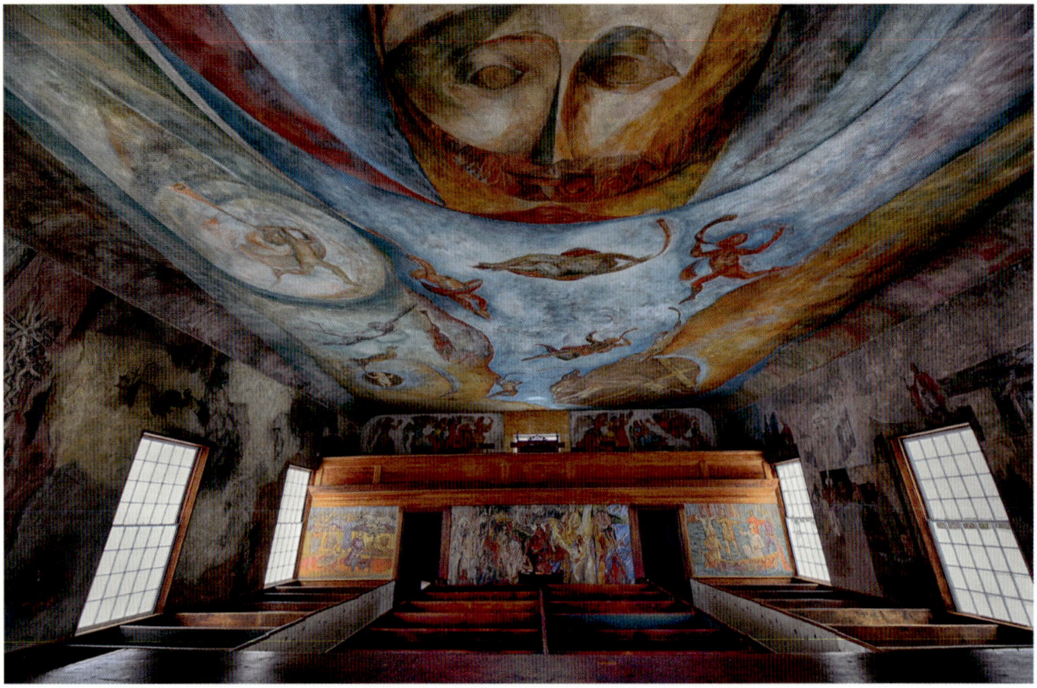

A view from the pulpit looking out toward the congregation pews. The massive face of Christ dubbed "Godhead" sees all.

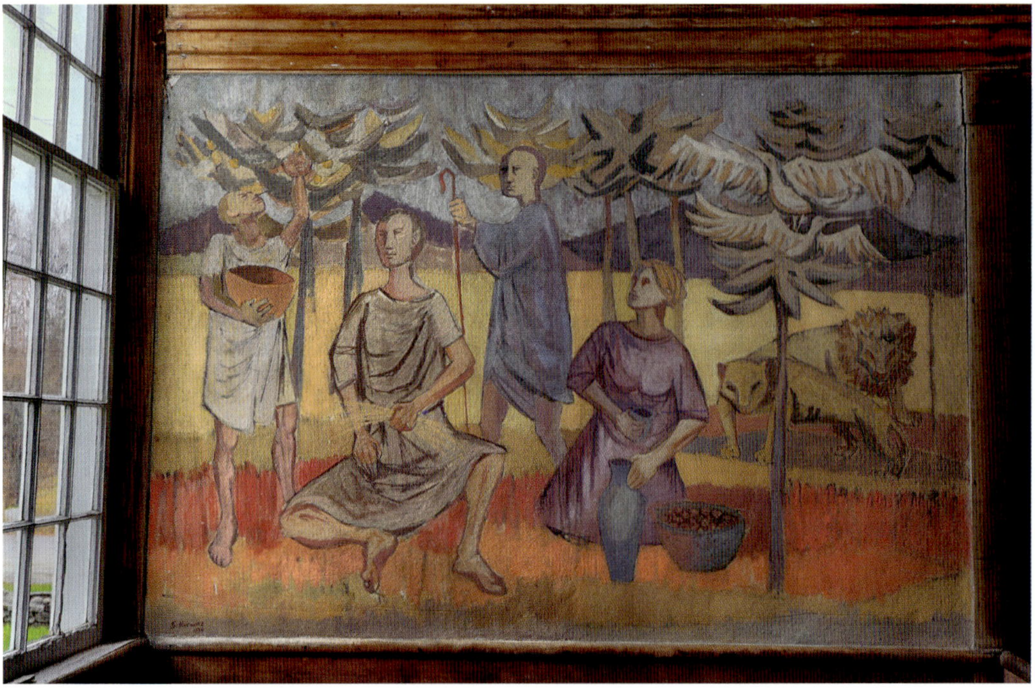

Artists used natural light to enhance the creation of their works. This sixty-six-year-old fresco is as vibrant as the day it was created against the light of the window.

There are many illustrated depictions of various biblical writings from Moses at Mount Sinai to this reimagining of The Last Supper.

A scene depicting the burning bush from Exodus 3:2 and a crippled Job are among the depictions on this fresco.

CONCLUSION

What is next for human evolution and our industrial and social practices? In the future, when we are powering cities with hydrogen, feeding people around the globe with nutritional, sustainable foods, and living in a stable climate, will the humans of tomorrow look back at our lithium batteries, electric cars, and acres of solar panels, and marvel at the primitive ingenuity that we currently view as state of the art? I suspect they will, and I suspect there will be people like me running around trying to document the last solar panel or windmill before it is taken down.

It is true we cannot save them all and preserve each thing from our past. We have limited space on this planet of ours and that space is only getting smaller. Yet, it is a shame that these places fall away, get ruined, replaced, or just pushed aside.

It is enjoyable to take a step back and consider the way things used to be. It was certainly an era when you had to work hard to survive and succeed, not unlike our contemporary world, but it also seems as though it were a time when people really had a sense of community and were forced to come together in the spirit of comradery and societal well-being.

Technology has now replaced our need to gather in social groups. We can message or follow each other on social media platforms, and we no longer rely on the telegraph office down at the station to bring us the news of the day. We just turn on the television using electricity we do not even think about while drinking milk delivered to our homes by a milkman.

Wait, what?

At the risk of contradicting my entire book, here in our contemporary society we do still have a milkman, but it is now a milk person, and milk is delivered not by milk truck or train, but by Door Dash or Uber Eats. The milk can now be ordered on our phones and brought to our door without ever interacting with another human being.

Social media seems rather a hypocritical term when we consider how it eliminates the need for us to act on our innate social needs. It remains to be seen by explorers of the future if this will result in us having less ability to come together as one community voice or if it will strengthen our bond as a society.

Dry goods, post office, groceries—all things offered on this store façade built in 1898. An 1899 local newspaper stated the new establishment was "filled with the latest assortment of goods ... during the busy season, their large business requires the services of six and eight clerks."[1] That is a radical departure from our contemporary shopping experience where we no longer even have clerks but instead use self-checkouts in many large retail outlets.

REFERENCES/ENDNOTES

Introduction

1. Wikipedia contributors. "Divco," *Wikipedia*, November 15, 2022, en.wikipedia.org/wiki/Divco.

Chapter 1

1. Richmond's Business and Industry. "The Wayne Works," *Morrisson-Reeves Library*, November 16, 2022, mrlinfo.org/history/business/wayneworks.htm
2. Buffalo Architecture and History. "Antique and Classic Car Show," October 15, 2022, buffaloah.com/a/notting/25/2015/auto.html
3. Northeast Firenews. "Plymouth Fire Department," November 2, 2022, firenews.org/mass/p/plymouth/plymouth.html
4. Ferrara. "About," November 14, 2022, ferrarafire.com/about/

Chapter 3

1. Neff, A. "Plan floated, but boat still aground in Hampden," *Bangor Daily News*. August 17, 2011, bangordailynews.com/2011/08/16/news/bangor/plan-floated-but-boat-still-aground-in-hampden/
2. NavSource Online. "Service Ship Photo Archive," December 1, 2022, navsource.org/archives/14/31414.htm

Chapter 4

1. Nett, B. "A Day in the Life of Bob Roberts," *CP Rail News*. Volume 18 No. 6. (Calgary, Canada: Canadian Pacific 1988)

Chapter 5

1. Bureau of Parks and Lands. "The Eagle Lake & West Branch Railroad," *Maine Department of Agriculture, Conservation & Forestry*. maine.gov/dacf/parks/discover_history_explore_nature/history/allagash/index.shtml
2. Barker, A. "Lacroix's Legacy," *North Maine Woods, Inc.* northmainewoods.org/images/pdf/lacroix.pdf
3. Bureau of Parks and Lands. "Churchill Depot," *Maine Department of Agriculture, Conservation & Forestry*. maine.gov/dacf/parks/discover_history_explore_nature/history/allagash/chdepot.shtml
4. Bureau of Parks and Lands. "The Eagle Lake & West Branch Railroad," Maine *Department of Agriculture, Conservation & Forestry*. maine.gov/dacf/parks/discover_history_explore_nature/history/allagash/index.shtml
5. Bureau of Parks and Lands. "The Eagle Lake Tramway," *Maine Department of Agriculture, Conservation & Forestry*. maine.gov/dacf/parks/discover_history_explore_nature/history/allagash/tram.shtml

Chapter 6

Cooper, B. "The Belfast & Moosehead Lake Railroad," *Central Pacific Railroad Photographic History Museum*. cprr.org/Museum/BMLRR/

Chapter 7

1. Burns, A. "Bangor and Aroostook Railroad: Serving Northern Maine," *American-Rails.com*. american-rails.com/aroostook.html

Chapter 8

1. Peters, B., *Maine Central Railroad Company: A Story of Success and Independence* (Portland, Maine: Maine Central Railroad Company 1976)
2. Burns, A. "Maine Central Railroad: The Pine Tree Route," *American-Rails.com*. american-rails.com/mec.html
3. Macdougall, W. *The Old Somerset Railroad: A Lifetime for Northern Mainers* (Camden, Maine: *Down East Books* 2000)

Chapter 9

1. "Brooks," *The Republican Journal*, Volume 93 No. 43, pp. 6 (Belfast, Maine: The Republican Journal, 1921)
2. *A Broad Expanse of Lake Sebasticook* (Newport, Maine: Arthur W. Lander, Printer 1914)
3. Gibbs, P., "Maine Coast Railroad Going Out of Business" *Boothbay Register*, Vol. 124, No. 41, (Boothbay Harbor, Maine: Boothbay Register 2000)

Part II

Chapter 10

1. "1870-1920 The End of the Ocean Highway," *Maine History Online*. mainememory.net/sitebuilder/site/905/page/1316/display

Chapter 11

1. "Berst-Forster-Dixfield Division, Timber Unit Records, Identifier," *Diamond Match Company* SpC MS 0050

   'Vintage Aerial, Film Roll 8', *Penobscot County,* Photo 8-MCPE-27, 1963

'Maine Industries 1939', *Maine Department of Labor and Industry*, All Bureau of Labor Standards Documents. Paper 180 1944

2. Ohm, R. "Buyer's Ideas Far From Run-of-the-mill," *The Portland Press Herald*, November 12, 2012 (Portland, Maine: Portland Press Herald, 2012)
3. Ohm, R. "Buyer's Ideas Far From Run-of-the-mill," *The Portland Press Herald*, November 12, 2012 (Portland, Maine: Portland Press Herald, 2012)
4. Isaac, S. "There is still plenty of life-and afterlife in the North Vassalboro Olde Mill," *The Town Line*, October 30, 2019 (South China, Maine: The Town Line 2019)

Chapter 12

1. Kelley, K. "Stonehenge of Maine?" *President of the Searsport Historical Society*, Personal communication, October 15, 2022

Part III

Chapter 13

1. Staff Writer Portsmouth Herald, "Old Alfred jailhouse saw inmates come and go," *Seacoastonline*, August 2, 2012 (New York: Gannett Media Corp. 2012)
2. Thaxter, C., "A Memorable Murder," *The Atlantic Monthly*, Vol. 35, pp. 602-615, (Washington, DC: The Atlantic Monthly 1875)
3. Robinson, J., "Anatomy of an Ax Murder," *Murde74rpedia.org*, murderpedia.org/male.W/w/wagner-louis.htm

Chapter 14

1. Morton, E., "Historical Address of the Town of Jackson" (Waterville, Maine: Mail Publishing Co., Printers 1912)
2. "Lamoine, First Baptist Church," *National Register of Historic Places-Listings*, Maine an Encyclopedia, maineanencyclopedia.com/lamoine/
3. Feldberg, S., "A historic Vassalboro church that was focus of months-long dispute is demolished," *CentralMaine.com*, July 27, 2022 (Waterville, Maine: Morning Sentinel 2022)
4. Chase, H., "The Early History of the Town of Dexter," *The Eastern Gazette Historical Souvenir*, Supplement to Issue of August 4, 1904, Volume 43, pp. 11 (Dexter, Maine: Eastern Gazette 1904)
5. Clifford, P,. *Town of Dixmont*, Maine Employee. Personal communication, November 9, 2022
6. "Grange, The," *Maine: An Encyclopedia*, February 23, 2013 maineanencyclopedia.com/grange-the/

Chapter 15

1. "South Solon Meeting House," southsolonmeetinghouse.org

Conclusion

1. "Lawrence Brothers store," *Lubec Historical Society*, mainememory.net/artifact/28735